P.I.P.E.L.I.N.E.
TURN YOUR PASSION INTO PERPETUAL PROFIT

BY DR. SANDRA COLTON-MEDICI

PASSION P.I.P.E.L.I.N.E.

The 8-step method to turn your passion into a perpetual payoff.
Copyright © 2020 Sandra Colton-Medici
All rights reserved. No part of this book may be reproduced or
distributed in any printed or electronic form without permission.
Cover, contents, and chapter images: canva.com

WWW.SANDRACOLTONMEDICI.COM

Copyright 2020 by Sandra Colton-Medici

All rights reserved. Passion P.I.P.E.L.I.N.E. Printed and bound in the United States of America. No part of this work may be reproduced in any form or by any electronic or mechanical means including information storage and retrieval systems without permission in writing from the publisher, except by a reviewer, who may quote brief passages in a review.

Published by Pinstriped Publishing
A Division of Original Girl, LLC
P.O. Box 824, Hollywood, CA 90078

For more works by Sandra Colton-Medici go online to www.SandraColtonMedici.com.

ISBN 978-0-578-74004-1
Library of Congress Control Number: 2020914879
First printing: September 2020

Colton-Medici, Sandra
    Passion P.I.P.E.L.I.N.E.: turn your passion into perpetual profit / Sandra Colton-Medici - 1st ed.
    p. cm.

Edited by Sandra Colton-Medici

The scanning, uploading, and distribution of this book via the Internet or via any other means without the permission of the publisher is illegal and punishable by law. Please purchase only authorized electronic editions and do not participate in or encourage electronic piracy of copyrightable materials. Your support of the author's rights is appreciated.

While the author has made every effort to provide accurate information at the time of publication, neither the publisher nor the author assumes any responsibility for errors, or for any changes that occur after publication. Further, the publisher does not have any control over and does not assume any responsibility for any third-party websites or their content. The author, publisher, and copyright holder assume no responsibility for any injury, loss, or damage sustained or caused as a consequence of the use and application of this book.

ABOUT THE AUTHOR

Sandra Colton-Medici holds a Doctor of Education, with a specific emphasis on Organizational Change & Leadership, from the University of Southern California. Her doctoral dissertation explored e-commerce marketing strategies and methods used to target online consumers. Sandra's background includes teaching as a Lecturer of Dance Studies at USC Glorya Kaufman School of Dance. Her latest work is a curation of moving images that demonstrate how dance impacts pop culture on DanceAndPopCulture.com. Sandra will be debuting her first children's book in Summer 2021 and most recently launched her self-paced online program, Course Sweetener, to help people break free of their 9 to 5 jobs and work from anywhere. Sandra's academic achievements include a Doctor of Education (USC, 2019), Master's Degree in Communication Management (USC, 2015), Bachelor's Degree in Sociology (University of Oregon, 2000) and VOGUE Fashion Certificate (Condé Nast College of Fashion & Design, 2014) in London, UK.

Sandra appeared on Lifetime's hit show *Dance Moms*, was a top finalist on Season 1 of FOX's *So You Think You Can Dance*, has performed on *The Tonight Show with Jay Leno* singing backup for both Paulina Rubio and Katharine McPhee and danced in music videos for Snoop Dogg, Justin Timberlake, Chelo, The Game, Katharine McPhee, Raphael Saadiq, Marie Serenholt, Cascada and Too Short. Her resume also includes work as an actor in *The Day The Earth Stood Still*, *Black is King*, commercials for Fruit of the Loom, Subway & Nationwide Insurance as well as publishing/editing magazines, books, and articles on dance.

Sandra is the creator of Icons of Online Movement, an annual virtual conference and event series that aims to help dance and fitness individuals create, promote, and monetize their online businesses. Her *Level Up* Instagram Live chat series was the impetus for Sandra's forthcoming book entitled, "Digital Literacy and Marketing Strategies for Successful Careers in the Performing Arts," due out in 2021.

WWW.SANDRACOLTONMEDICI.COM

DEDICATION

This is dedicated to my loved ones who sacrifice daily to assist me with my dreams. I am forever grateful that you support me. To my husband and two beautiful daughters, thank you from the bottom of my heart.
I love you!

CONTENTS

FIND YOUR PASSION
0

PRACTICE
1

INVENTIVENESS
2

PURSUE
3

EXCITEMENT
4

LIVE
5

INSPIRED
6

NEGOTIATE
7

ENERGY
8

WWW.SANDRACOLTONMEDICI.COM

FIND YOUR PASSION

0

FIND YOUR PASSION

I wanted to write this book because I felt like there are so many people who have untapped passion. I feel like there are droves of people with this, and they would live their passion, if they just had a swift kick in the butt. To me, life is way too short to let it pass you by without actually putting in the work, and doing the homework necessary to get the results you want to achieve.

This topic reminds me of that movie, *Forrest Gump*, where Tom Hanks' character said, "Life is like a box of chocolates. You never know what you're going to get." And in my head, I'm thinking, well, sometimes you really do know what you're going to get. If you have a passion and seek to exercise your talent and abilities, and the skills you know, then you know what you will get because the end result will be indicative of what effort you put into it. So you will see what you will get, you just don't know how long it will take to get there. You also don't know how many opportunities you will need to get through or change from one thing to another to find your way.

An excellent example of this is the attempts it takes when someone practices their basketball shot. They know that they are developing a skill that ultimately should result in getting the ball through the hoop. I feel like when I sat down to write this book, I really was oblivious to what would come out of my mouth. That is because I decided to speak the book into my phone to see what would happen. I have never used the dictation function on my phone, but I felt like sometimes you can't just type it out. This time I wanted to be in the moment. So this is what I've done in creating this book.

I want this book to speak to you. I want it to read like you hear my voice just kind of tickling your ear, saying, "You can do anything you want. You can be anything you want. You can live your passion if you want."

I was sitting in my living room with my mom just yesterday, and I was trying to come up with something that was really important to me, but also extremely important to the people who I've worked with, and people who I am yet to work with. The motivational drive and underlying passion that people have to do what they do is undeniable. You can't teach it. You can't wish it upon them. You have to have that thing for yourself, whatever that thing is inside of you.

Now, in talking to my mom, I have always kind of noticed that I'm passionate about a lot of things. I'm sure just like you, you have many things you would love to do and are passionate about. The hard part for me, sometimes, is that I get really caught up in that thing that I wanted to do today, and then the next day, if I didn't get it done, I have something new that I'd like to do. So, I just keep adding and adding and adding to my plate. That is a character trait that I often find in extremely artistic people and driven people. You want a lot. You think a lot. You have the energy to do things that other people would probably put off until other times.

Focusing on your passion sometimes dissipates because there are so many directions you would like to pursue. I created this book to help people really follow their passion and create a pipeline that will help people navigate their passion to fruition, whatever it is. Passion P.I.P.E.L.I.N.E. is the name of this book. Naming things is important to me because it makes them real. It's like writing something down. It makes it come to life on paper. That, to me, is the ultimate zing. If I can write something down and see it on paper, that makes it real to me. It can be an idea for a script, a measure of a song, a move to a dance routine, a module for a course, a technology hack, or a simple note to self. These are ways that I find myself sitting down and writing down what I'd like to do, where I see myself going, and putting it to paper the way I see my future.

Passion is not perfect. Passion is persistent. Passion can be powerful. When I decided that I would make the word pipeline an acronym for my 8-step method put forth in this book, I wanted to make sure that people understood that it can be combined or it can be separated. The pipeline can be detailed the way you envision it for yourself. How do you see your future?

The **Passion P.I.P.E.L.I.N.E.** 8-step Method:
Practice
Inventiveness
Pursue
Excitement
Live
Inspired
Negotiate
Energy

All of the actions in the 8-step Passion P.I.P.E.L.I.N.E. Method are ways in which you can utilize your passion for pushing yourself to the next level. I wanted to break down each step so that you can create different approaches in your life to follow the Passion P.I.P.E.L.I.N.E. Method (PPM). The PPM is meant to be a road map for you to listen to yourself, trust in your decision-making skills, believe that you are the master of your domain, and finally put to paper your next step to an amazing life. So, let's start with the first step.

PRACTICE

1

PRACTICE
PASSION P.I.P.E.L.I.N.E.

Practice is the first step in the 8-step Passion P.I.P.E.L.I.N.E. Method (PPM). Most people say that practice makes perfect, but I had an employer one time tell me, "Practice makes perfect for some people, but perfect practice makes perfect in my book." And I trust that his statement is very true.

It is vital that if you have a passion that you practice, number one, what you preach, but also that you practice that skill, whatever it is that you're passionate about.

It can be playing tennis, track and field, or professional hot dog eating, whatever it is, you name it, it's essential to keep that passion in practice.

Passion is not your enemy. Passion can be a saving grace in a time of need. It can be the one thing that gets you through, and it can inspire others to pursue their dreams.

I like to practice many different things that I love. Some of those things include painting, dancing, singing, acting, makeup tutorials, editing, publishing, and the list can go on and on. Even if the top thing that you love to do, you don't do very well, you should probably practice it and make this so-so skill just as good as your best skill.

INVENTIVENESS
PASSION P.I.P.E.L.I.N.E.

Inventiveness is the next step in the 8-step Passion P.I.P.E.L.I.N.E. Method (PPM). I use this word because I believe that people who invent things are really crucial to the way that we function in society.

Look at the Post-It®. Look at Dyson air conditioners and vacuum cleaners. Look at Amazon®. Look at Facebook. Look at the invention of the automobile. Look at the Frisbee. Haha! Yes, even the Frisbee. These are some of the most amazing ideas and concepts to ever come into the marketplace.

So, how do you become an inventor if you don't know how to make anything or have no ideas on how to create something new? The inventiveness that I am talking about is always inside of you. Being an inventor does not mean that you have to create a new sticky glue or some sort of digital domain. It does mean that you need to always practice working on your craft to continuously move it forward. That means being progressive in your field and never ever ever ever feeling like you need to copy someone else to make a name for yourself.

Being a creator is extremely important because your ideas in the marketplace may, like I said before, inspire someone else to create and invent as well. Practice your skills and those skills will become a creative outlet for whatever it is that you are in love with doing. Whether it is creating new businesses or writing songs, you're practicing and working that muscle of being an idea-maker, being a content creator, and putting those ideas out into the world.

PURSUE
PASSION P.I.P.E.L.I.N.E.

Pursue is the next step in the 8-step Passion P.I.P.E.L.I.N.E. Method (PPM). I like to use this word as my push motivation. It's important not to feel stagnant in any kind of creative process.

For some people, there are motivating factors, for example, you have been assigned a project, and you have a deadline. For many, with their own personal passion, there is no deadline. **So YOU are your own motivator**. That means that you are the person responsible for the outcomes if there are going to be any. YOU are the person who is going to move the needle. YOU are the one who will pursue your passion and go after your dreams.

What will it take for you to choose the next step on your passion and pursue your dream? Sometimes this is the hardest question to answer. The first question is, what is your passion? The next question is, are you any good at it? And then the next issue would be, why haven't you done anything about it yet?

I asked myself this very question when I was dancing professionally for Mary J. Blige in a skeleton crew for her upcoming tour. And instead of sitting on my laurels and not doing anything about it, I decided to write a book. This is the perfect example of pursuing passion. I had never written a book before. I had never really wanted to write a book. I had no idea what it took to write a book. I just knew that I was a good writer. I knew that I had excellent editing skills and good interviewing skills. I didn't have the software that I needed to get it done, so I bought it.

Oh actually, let me back up, I think I swiped it from my friend. I know it's going to sound so crazy. My friend had the software, and he agreed to meet me in a parking lot in Seattle, Washington. Just think about this scene. We both drove into the parking lot, rolled down our windows, and he threw it into my car. He made it seem as if we were part of a ridiculous undercover drop or sting operation where we switched briefcases. Clearly, I didn't know what was going on, and yes, the software was licensed for use. It was like a springboard that allowed me to start the journey writing my first book.

That was in 2007, almost 13 years ago. After writing my first book, I went on to edit and publish a magazine, create my online course, and speak this book into existence for you, that you are reading right now. And, then of course, in between all of that, I was performing and doing a lot of different television and film work, in addition to commercials, and music videos for artists like Justin Timberlake, Rihanna, and many more.

The reason I bring that up is that many people have told me, "Well, I have a lot of passion for things, and I'm pretty creative when it comes to what I like to do, but I really don't have the time to pursue that because I'm busy." Or the excuse will be because they have family obligations or I don't think they are an expert, because who's gonna listen to me? mentality.

To that, I say, never ever think that about yourself. If you want to pursue something, you will find the time. I am going to say that again. If you're going to create something, you will find the time. If something motivates you and drives you enough, you will find the time to do it. As I'm speaking this book into my phone, my husband is reading his mint condition books, because that is his passion. We have two young daughters, and they are both asleep, and I am speaking my book into my phone as my passion and he is reading his book that he does not get to read during the day because that is part of his passion. Now, I can tell you to pursue your dreams, pursue your goals, and find what makes you happy until I'm blue in the face. Until you are ready and committed to making your passion your number one thing, I can't help.

I have found that people can tell me, "Oh you're really good at that, you should do that," or, "Do you know you have so much talent in XYZ, why don't you write a course about that?" And to me, unless it moves me to the core, and it speaks to me, I'm not going to put my time and energy into it. That means not pursuing it.

So, that's why I say to you, YOU have to want it. I think my mom used to tell me that too. When I was three years old, I would go to my dance class and she would tell me, "You have to want this, I can't want it for you." So I'm going to tell you the same thing right now. YOU need to want it and YOU need to pursue it for yourself.

As an admissions advisor for a few different liberal arts colleges, I was able to work with, advise, and mentor students. One of the biggest things that I would encounter while speaking with students and parents was a high level of passion. The student passion and parental passion were sometimes on the same page, and sometimes not. But if the student was not coming from a home that had a lot of support, their passion is the first thing that they questioned. I would always tell them, "Do not ever give up your passion. If that is where you see yourself in life and what you want to pursue then go after it." I want you to hear the same message. If it is what you are meant to do, go after it.

EXCITEMENT
PASSION P.I.P.E.L.I.N.E.

Excitement is the next step in the 8-step Passion P.I.P.E.L.I.N.E. Method (PPM). I like to use this word as my *let's do this* type of motivation. It's important to feel - and have a sort of impact on one's self - an internal fun meter.

Now the pursuit of happiness is not guaranteed in the Passion P.I.P.E.L.I.N.E. I highlight that you are pursuing excitement, because I come from an artistic background, and I need to be fulfilled. I want to fill my cup. I want to be able to say, "Wow, that is exciting!" Or, "Really?! Oh my goodness. I need to do that again." I want to experience that. What was that? I want to know that I can find little moments of excitement in all that I do, because that is going to keep me going and keep me pursuing that creativeness and inventiveness and keep on practicing those skills to perfection.

Now, what is exciting? That is all going to depend on you and what you find appealing. Excitement and pursuing excitement may make you have to find additional time to set aside from your family and friends, which may change your family and friends over time. Many people who follow their passion do not know how to balance their time. Having a balanced work/life schedule is not a priority for many people who follow their passion. So my one caveat to the Passion P.I.P.E.L.I.N.E. is to make sure that you are organized and focusing on prioritizing passion and purpose. Make sure that you're at peace with where you put your focus.

For a long time, I prioritized performing and my passion for show business and the entertainment industry, over my personal relationships. I found that over the years, I was more fulfilled when I was on stage. I had boyfriends. I had long-term relationships, but nothing was as exciting or as important as living my best life on stage.

I missed a lot of family engagements. I missed a lot of birthday parties, Christmas gatherings, Thanksgiving gatherings, and many other events. My mom was always happy for me, because I was doing what I wanted to do. And it made me happy too, for a very very long time. Until one day, I looked up from what I was doing, and I realized that I wanted more for myself, as far as having my own family.

I didn't go out and look for a family. I didn't go out and search for my husband, either. He just happened along at the right time, and he is the love of my life. I am grateful that the decisions that I made in going to London and then to France allowed us to find one another. It really is so random how things worked out. But it's not always that way for a lot of people. I caution passionate people who are trying to figure out exactly how to navigate this whole thing called life. Ensure that you are at peace with your outside commitments and take those into account when you are pursuing your dream. You need to either include them, don't include them, or try to find a happy balance in the in between.

LIVE
PASSION P.I.P.E.L.I.N.E.

Live is the next step in the 8-step Passion P.I.P.E.L.I.N.E. Method (PPM). I like to use this word as my don't forget, you're the captain of your own ship, realization moment. It's important to give yourself the freedom to take chances.

If you are pursuing excitement through your practice of inventiveness, then that means that you are living, which is the next step in the passion pipeline. I think, at the beginning of this book, I said something about living your best life and that is exactly what I want YOU to do. I live like nobody else is watching what's happening. You can do this too!

I know we are all on social media and everybody can see everything that's happening in everyone's life. Really, they are only seeing what you show them. You are in charge of your own life. You are in the driver's seat of where you are going. You are the one who is making sure that your cup is full 100% of the time. I like to combine Live with the next step in the Passion P.I.P.E.L.I.N.E., which is Inspired - Live Inspired. To really feel free to take chances is to find yourself letting go. If you are opening up to external possibilities, seek a way to explore and undo some of the binding that has been self-imposed. By doing this, you may find your true inspiration.

INSPIRED

6

INSPIRED
PASSION P.I.P.E.L.I.N.E.

Inspired is the next step in the 8-step Passion P.I.P.E.L.I.N.E. Method (PPM). I like to use this word as a sort of *eye of the tiger* measurement. It's important not to identify true inspiration through experiences but also reflection.

It is great to say you have **lived**. It is even better to say you are **inspired by life**. That means that you are taking something from a museum and internalizing it, analyzing it, and feeling like you got something from it. An example could be that you are traveling the world and having cultural experiences that enhance your well-being. Another example could be that you are merely resting at night and finding ways to ease your brain through guided meditation. I find that, for myself, I am inspired by so much that I need to unplug to feel like I can recharge my body and my mind.

To see and feel additional inspiration, try to look in places you would otherwise stop short and think twice before exploring.

There are passionate people out there, and you are probably one of them who can vouch for your brain just never shutting off. Your mind is continually running, pulling in, and aggregating information. Inspiration is coming from all around you - at all times. It is great to experience a rush of excitement, a feeling of accomplishment, or a notion that you are part of this existential experience.

It also can be very overwhelming. So when I say, **live inspired**, you need to live in a place where you can receive inspiring words of wisdom, and pieces of information of artistic relevance. Receive inspirational gifts, but also create balance with YOUR inspirational output to the world. Balance your being inspired in with your gift of inspiration.

NEGOTIATE
PASSION P.I.P.E.L.I.N.E.

Negotiate is the next step in the 8-step Passion P.I.P.E.L.I.N.E. Method (PPM). I like to use this word as my give and get guidance. It's important to remember that there may be a give and take process to your passion.

You are already practicing your passion by just reading this e-book. You are looking for a way to zero in on what you want to do and find a way to get all of that passionate, inspiring inventiveness to the world. This is where you need to negotiate what you feel is your priority.

Ask yourself the following questions:
What is your endgame?
What will be the most satisfying at this moment?
What are you seeking to complete?
Who are you?
Where do you want to go?
When you can answer these questions - that's where you begin your negotiation.

You are going to write down your answers, pen to paper. Negotiating your priority is fundamental to actually achieving your goals. Passionate people with many many many different buckets to fill, usually only fill each bucket a little bit. You're never filling one bucket completely full.

When I was first signed to DDO Talent agency in Los Angeles, California, back in 2002, I also was interested in singing. I had an agent, and that particular agency also represented singers. I met with the person who was in charge of the singing department, and he said to me,

"You are a good dancer. You need to focus on building your resume through dance. After you have notoriety through dance, then you can parlay your dance skills into a singing career." I was like, "Yeah, right! I just want to sing, and dance, and do everything." But, he was right. And, I did it the way he said I should.

An excellent example of this is Jessica Simpson. She was first out on the scene as a singer. She did not begin her shoe line until way later in her career. If she had come out as a handbag lady in addition to her singing career, people probably wouldn't have taken her very seriously. But, she clearly has a passion for music and fashion. It is essential to know that she's good at both. She is not just kind of good at one and kind of good at the other. That is what I meant about filling your buckets. She's filling her music bucket full, and she's filling her fashion bucket all the way full. She may not have done an album recently, but she definitely was at the top of her game when she was producing music. You can go from one passion project to another, but you must establish yourself in one field before deciding that you will be an expert in four different fields. That is what I'm talking about when I say, "You need to negotiate your passion."

ENERGY
PASSION P.I.P.E.L.I.N.E.

Energy is the next step in the 8-step Passion P.I.P.E.L.I.N.E. Method (PPM). I like to use this word as my supercharge my life measurement. It's essential to place your energy where it will be most effective and serve your overall purpose.

Negotiating your passion begins with YOU. It doesn't start with your audience. It begins with you asking yourself internally, how much you can take on, and how much you can give of yourself to each individual Passion Project. If you can go to medical school, be pregnant with triplets, have a one-on-one coaching business, and decide to take on an in-home daycare with 20 children -- I mean, that's a lot. I'm not saying that women can't do it, I am saying that it's a lot to take on when you're trying to be 150% at multiple things.

When you are looking at your Passion P.I.P.E.L.I.N.E., and you have practiced your skills, worked on your creative inventiveness through that practice, and decided that you would pursue your passion, focus on what excites you by living inspired and negotiating your energy toward that space. Whatever that is for you, make it happen!

That's where the last step of the Passion P.I.P.E.L.I.N.E. comes in. Energy is part of your Passion P.I.P.E.L.I.N.E., and that means that YOU are deciding what matters. You are deciding where you are going to put your energy and your focus. For example, you might have a product or offer a service, and you decide that your focus will be with philanthropy or a charity. Wherever your passion lies, go back to what I stated regarding making peace with those around you. Make sure that you have a balanced work/life situation. You will have to negotiate where your energy lies best. For me, my energy was best placed pursuing my dance career first. After dance, I was able to pursue singing, acting, publishing, editing, digital strategy, education, academic teaching, and creating online courses. There is so much that I have accomplished because I prioritized those passion projects and negotiated with myself exactly which one I should do first, second, third, fourth, and fifth.

I know sometimes you might have something come up out of the blue. An opportunity just presents itself and lands itself right there in your lap. You will need to say to yourself, "Do I take it advantage of this? Is this part of my Passion P.I.P.E.L.I.N.E.? Is this something that is going to fulfill me for a short term? Or, is it going to be something that I need to add to my plan of where I put my energy?"

You can only have a certain amount passion projects running 100% at any given time. But, you only have a certain amount of energy. If you're young, have vitality, and are just kicking and screaming with tons of buzzy buzzy feelings going on, well - yay for you! But having passion is generally draining.

Use your creativity and inventiveness and put your skills to work by pursuing your passion. You will need to negotiate your energy with yourself and with your family, friends, or whoever is your support network. For example, when I am low on the power I need to figure out what will reinvigorate my passion, I call upon my support network to remind me where I've communicated my passion lies. You will have to come back to different parts of your pipeline to make sure that you are living inspired and practicing your inventiveness. You will check in to affirm that you are pursuing excitement to feel fulfilled enough to bring your energy level up to perform at your optimum level.

You will need these periodic checks to complete the tasks or goals that you set out to fulfill.

I created the **Passion P.I.P.E.L.I.N.E.** because, like me, I know that YOU have so much to give. You are just bursting at the seams with so many ideas and so many gifts that you need a place to organize what you want to do and express how you want to accomplish it. You want to keep your glass full instead of half empty.

I hope that you can always come back to the Passion P.I.P.E.L.I.N.E. and understand that maybe the skill that you aren't 100% at, you can go back to the first part of the book where you focus on practice. And then, perhaps you don't know where you need to go next, and you come back to pursue an element to really figure out what you want to do. And maybe you are rundown because you're seeking so many avenues that are fulfilling that you just cannot hold focus. I hope that you come back to the negotiate and negotiating your energy portion of the Passion P.I.P.E.L.I.N.E. so that you understand how to best serve YOU and your personal core.

I hope that this book helps you, drives and motivates you to continuously refresh your soul through utilizing the Passion P.I.P.E.L.I.N.E. to obtain your future goals. As a business owner, as a mom, as a professor, as someone who believes in YOU, I know that there are so many things that hold people back. Fear is one of those things. Fear of the unknown precisely. That is what holds many people back from moving forward in the pursuit part of the pipeline.

Fear is also something that has a hand in ensuring that people do not live inspired. People believe that living inspired means that you have to have a lot of money. **YOU DO NOT HAVE TO HAVE A LOT OF MONEY TO HAVE PASSION**. You do not have to have a lot of money to go to a free art museum and look at paintings by amazing artists. You do not have to have money to stand outside and be inspired by street performers at Venice Beach or the Santa Monica Pier. You do not have to have money to go to the library and read books about everything and anything.

I want to put the challenge to you, write down your ideas, and to put them to paper to get your passion out in a visual format so that you can see it. If you are not a person who typically visualizes things, I want you to become a person that is. Now you do not actually have to see to be visualizing your passion. Many people are musicians, scriptwriters, or business owners who are visually impaired, but they still have a vision.

Once written down, you can change it. You can morph it into something even better by editing it. You can have someone else critique or enhance it. There are so many things you can do once your passion or ideas are out of your body and on a piece of paper.

I challenge you to write down your passion and make sure that you send me a note to let me know that you are working on your passion now. I want to see what you are up to and where you are headed. Use the following hashtags and tag me on my social handles @sandracoltonmedici #PassionPIPELINE

NOTES

NOTES

NOTES

NOTES

NOTES

NOTES

NOTES

NOTES

NOTES

NOTES

NOTES

NOTES

NOTES

NOTES

NOTES

NOTES

NOTES

THE END

WWW.SANDRACOLTONMEDICI.COM

www.ingramcontent.com/pod-product-compliance
Lightning Source LLC
Chambersburg PA
CBHW071416290426
44108CB00014B/1847